# SCHIRMER'S LIBRARY
## OF MUSICAL CLASSICS

Vol. 1662

# JOHANNES BRAHMS

## Variations On A Theme by Haydn

### For Piano

ISBN 978-0-7935-2058-9

**G. SCHIRMER, Inc.**

DISTRIBUTED BY
**HAL•LEONARD®**
CORPORATION
7777 W. BLUEMOUND RD. P.O. BOX 13819 MILWAUKEE, WI 53213

T0050922

# Variations
## on a Theme by Josef Haydn
### Arranged for the Piano

Johannes Brahms

St. Anthony Chorale

**Andante**

**Var.1**
Andante con moto

**Var. 2**
Vivace

6

**Var. 3**
Con moto

**Var. 4**
**Andante**

### Var. 5
**Poco presto**

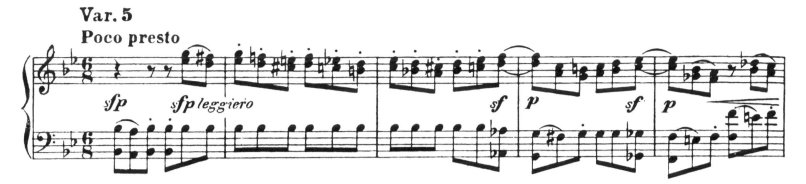

### Var. 6
#### Vivace

**Var. 7**
**Grazioso**

**Var. 8**
Poco presto

**Finale**
**Andante**

p *legàto*

(Basso ostinato)

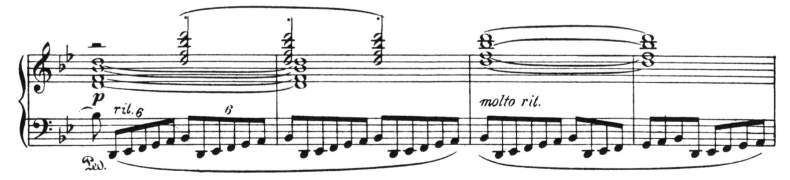